MW01056551

What is my Song?

Dennis Linn
Sheila Fabricant Linn
Matthew Linn SJ

Paulist Press
New York/Mahwah, New Jersey

ILLUSTRATIONS
BY
FRANCISCO
MIRANDA

Acknowledgments

We gratefully thank the following persons for their help and loving care in the preparation of this manuscript: Heather Campbell, Deb Deverell, Millie Dosh, Jean Marie Hiesberger, Glenna Rae Hovey, Sally Johnston, Julie Keith, Julie Lingle, Paul McMahon, Maureen Mulrooney, Jim Radde, Eleanor Sheehan, and Suzanne Weinberg.

Book design by Lynn Else
Jacket illustration by Francisco Miranda

Text copyright © 2005 by Dennis Linn, Sheila Fabricant Linn, and the Wisconsin Province of the Society of Jesus.
Illustrations by Francisco Miranda. Used with permission.

All rights reserved. No part of this book may be reproduced or transmitted in any form or by any means, electronic or mechanical, including photocopying, recording or by any information storage and retrieval system without permission in writing from the Publisher.

Library of Congress Cataloging-in-Publication Data

Linn, Dennis.
What is my song? / Dennis Linn, Sheila Fabricant Linn, Matthew Linn.
    p. cm.
ISBN 0-8091-6722-0 (alk. paper)
1. Vocation—Catholic Church—Juvenile literature. I. Linn, Sheila Fabricant. II. Linn, Matthew. III. Title.

BV4740.L56 2005
248.4—dc22

2004007387

Published by Paulist Press
997 Macarthur Boulevard
Mahwah, New Jersey 07430

www.paulistpress.com

Printed and bound in Mexico

For John

When did I begin to be me?

Was it on the day that I came out of my mama's tummy?

Was it on the day that I first went into her tummy and began to grow there?

My name is Deo. I live in East Africa. My people believe that I began to be me before I was born. I began to be me even before I began to grow inside my mama. I began to be me the very first time the idea of me came into my mama's heart.

When this happened, my mama went away by herself to sit under a tree.
She listened in her heart until she heard the special song of me.

Once she heard my song, she went back to the village and taught it to my papa. They sang it together, inviting me to come to them.

As I begin to grow inside her tummy, my mama often sings my song to me.

In the morning, she sings my song to me as she washes clothes in the river and lays them on the rocks to dry in the warm sun.

In the afternoon, she sings my song to me as she sifts millet.

In the evening, she sings my song to me with my papa as they watch the stars grow bright in the sky.

I feel so happy when at last she sings herself and me to sleep with my song.

When it is almost time for me to be born, my mama teaches my song to the other women of our village. When I come out of her tummy, the first thing I hear is the other women gathered around my mama, singing my song to me.

All the people of my village learn my song. Whenever I fall or hurt myself,
they sing it to me.

One night the wind blows a spark from our cooking fire
onto the roof of our grass thatched hut. I rush in to save my baby
brother. I carry him out, and all the people sing my song to me.

When my little sister falls into the river and I save her from drowning, they sing my song to me.

My song is about protecting people and keeping them from harm.

One day Matani, another boy in our village, takes my fishing net and tears it. I am very angry. Instead of telling him how angry I am, I throw a stone at him. The stone hits him on his face, and he falls to the ground. Matani's eyes are bleeding, and he cannot see.

I have forgotten that I am a protector. I do not know who I am anymore. I cannot remember my song.

Everyone in the village stops what they are doing. All the men stop working in the fields. All the women stop pounding grain. All the children stop playing their games.

In the middle of the village everyone makes a big circle around me. All together, they sing my song to me. They know who I am. Slowly, gradually, the song fills my heart and I remember, too. I am a protector.

I go to Matani's hut and I say, "I am sorry. If your eyes do not get better, I will be your eyes. I will lead you around the village and through the forest. I will fish for you. I will plant grain for you. I will protect you from danger."

I sing Matani's song to him. Gradually his eyes get better, and he can see again. So can I. I can see myself. I remember who I really am. I can hear my own song again. I am a protector.

The most important thing is that my song never leaves me even if I forget it for a while.

One afternoon I go out alone in the fishing boat. Suddenly the sky grows dark and stormy. The wind blows me out farther and farther away from land.

The water is very rough, and I cannot steer the boat over the big waves. I am so frightened I don't know what to do.

The other children are watching me from the shore. They begin to sing, louder and louder. They are singing my song. I feel strong again. I can steer the boat against the wind, back to where the other children are standing. I am safe.

When I become a man, the other men will sing my song to welcome me as one of them.

When I get married, all the people of my village will sing my song at my wedding.

And when I leave this world and go back to God, they will gather around my deathbed and sing my song to me for the last time.

Who are you?
Put your hand on your heart.
Can you feel your heart beating?
Take deep breaths, and listen deep inside your heart.
Can you hear your song?

A Note to Parents and Other Caregivers

This story is based upon a traditional African fable, which we first heard from Jack Kornfield.[1] We wrote this book for children because we believe that every child comes into this world knowing his or her own song. Parents who are listening, including adoptive parents, will often hear something of their child's song long before the child is born.

We don't need to teach our children their special purpose in life, as we would teach them to read or to ride a bike. Rather, we need to help them remember what they already know. How can we do this? Perhaps the best way is to remember and be true to our own special purpose in life, to our own song. Although it may be expressed in actions, such as protecting or teaching or writing,

our special purpose is first of all a way of being—it is "the spirit that animates" everything we do.[2] The three of us like to speak of it as our special way of giving and receiving love. At the end of each day we ask ourselves, "When was I most able to give and receive love?" The answer is usually those moments when we were most in tune with our song.

We have found several other questions to be useful in identifying our special purpose, and they are presented in our book *Healing the Purpose of Your Life* (Paulist Press, 1999). One of these questions might be especially helpful as we encourage our children to remember:

When in your life have you been so absorbed in something that time flew by without your noticing it? For example, as a child, what were you doing when you were called in for dinner and you came in late?[3]

When Sheila came in late for dinner, she was walking in the woods looking at stones and leaves of grass. Sheila's special purpose in life is to find the goodness in all of creation. She does this now through writing books and giving retreats that emphasize the goodness within each person. She also does it through nurturing the goodness of her and Denny's son, John. When Matt came in late for dinner, he was putting together puzzles. His special purpose in life involves finding the missing piece—whether in a theory, a person, or a culture. When we write books together, Matt often finds the missing piece. When Denny came in late for dinner, he was reading books about faraway places that he wanted to visit. His special purpose in life is to be a brother to everyone and everything, within and without. Many of the processes in our books for exploring the inner world, as well as many of our travels in the outer world, were inspired by Denny's desire to be a brother.

As we answer this question for ourselves, we are better able to hear our own song and gradually that of our children. For example, we notice that John comes in late for dinner because he is absorbed in dramatic, emergency rescues that he acts out with his toy fire trucks and ambulances. Perhaps, like Deo, John's special purpose in life involves protecting people and keeping them from harm. Whether by coming in late for dinner, by constantly returning to the same activity or interest, through recurring dreams or spontaneous outbursts of passionate excitement, or in some other way, our children will give us clues every day about why they came here. Then, whenever our children forget, we can help them remember their song.

1. Jack Kornfield, *A Path with Heart: A Guide Through the Perils and Promises of Spiritual Life* (New York: Bantam, 1993), p. 334, and *The Art of Forgiveness, Lovingkindness, and Peace* (New York: Bantam, 2002), p. 42.
2. We first heard our special purpose in life described as "the spirit that animates" everything we do from Herbert Alphonso, S.J. See his book *Discovering Your Personal Vocation* (Mahwah, NJ: Paulist Press, 2001), p. 26.
3. This question comes from Bernie Siegel's *How to Never Grow Old* (audiotape published by Sounds True Recordings, Boulder, CO, 1992).

Books and Tapes

The Linns are the authors of nineteen books, including *Healing of Memories, Healing Life's Hurts, Good Goats: Healing Our Image of God, Sleeping with Bread: Holding What Gives You Life,* and *Healing the Purpose of Your Life* (upon which this book is based). These books and others by the authors are available from Paulist Press, 997 Macarthur Blvd., Mahwah, NJ 07430. Phone orders: (800) 218-1903; fax orders: (800) 836-3161; website: www.paulistpress.com.

All of the Linns' materials, including audio- and videotapes, as well as courses, are available from Christian Video Library, 3914-A Michigan Ave., St. Louis, MO 63118; phone (314) 865-0729; fax (314) 773-3115. Videotapes may also be borrowed on a donation basis.

All materials are listed on their website, www.linnministries.org.

Books and Tapes in Spanish

Most of the Linns' books and tapes are available in Spanish. For more information, please contact Christian Video Library or go to www.linnministries.org.

Retreats and Conferences

For information about retreats and conferences by the authors, please call (970) 476-9235 or (314) 865-0729, or go to www.linnministries.org.